COLOR
your campus

IUPUI

INDIANA UNIVERSITY PURDUE UNIVERSITY INDIANAPOLIS

QUARRY BOOKS

AN IMPRINT OF
INDIANA UNIVERSITY PRESS

JOSEPH T. TAYLOR HALL (DETAIL). SAMANTHA PACIS, 2020

Quarry Books
an imprint of

Indiana University Press
Office of Scholarly Publishing
Herman B Wells Library 350
1320 East 10th Street
Bloomington, Indiana 47405 USA

iupress.org

First printing 2021

ISBN 978-0-253-05867-6 (pbk.)

COVER

CAMPUS CENTER
CONNOR STUMP, 2020

FOREWORD

We would like to thank the First Lady of Indiana University, Laurie Burns McRobbie, for suggesting "Color Your Campus– IUPUI." We would also like to thank IUPUI First Lady, Niloo Paydar, Chancellor Nasser H. Paydar, and his cabinet for their encouragement, feedback, and recommendations. Special thanks to Vice Chancellor for Community Engagement Amy Conrad Warner, Maureen Malone-Reed, Amy Hollrah, and Whitney Yoerger for their work on bringing together many aspects of the project. Most notably, we would like to thank Herron's Fine Arts Department Chair, Vance Farrow; faculty members Lowell Isaac, Kyle Latino, and Jingo de la Rosa; and all of the students of the drawing and illustration program for whom this has been an engaging, creative, and educational experience.

ABOUT HERRON

Founded in 1902, the Herron School of Art and Design is the premier accredited professional school of art and design in the state of Indiana and is part of the thriving urban campus of IUPUI. Herron has more than 50 full-time faculty serving 11 undergraduate and three graduate programs and a curriculum that prepares graduates to be leaders in a world that requires a unique combination of creativity, conceptual skills, and technical abilities. Herron is an engaged community and regional partner including five public galleries; youth and continuing education programs; and the Basile Center for Art, Design, and Public Life.

ABOUT IUPUI

As one of seven Indiana University campuses, IUPUI (Indiana University-Purdue University Indianapolis) is known as Indiana's premier urban research and health sciences institution and is dedicated to advancing the intellectual growth of the state of Indiana and its residents through research and creative activity, teaching, learning, and community engagement. Nationally ranked by *U.S. News & World Report, Forbes* and other notable publications, IUPUI has nearly 30,000 students enrolled in 17 schools, which offer more than 400 degrees. IUPUI awards degrees from both Indiana University and Purdue University.

INTRODUCTION

When the "Color Your Campus" project was presented to us, we wanted to use it as an opportunity to involve a group of students instead of commissioning a single artist. Since the semester was already well underway, the decision was made to use this project as part of the curriculum for juniors in Herron's Intermediate Illustration I course (HER-A 303). More than 40 students participated in the three sections of this class. We also approached a senior in our drawing and illustration program to create a cover image of the IUPUI Campus Center, a central and iconic building on our campus.

The coloring book offered a great opportunity to merge educational and creative coursework with a project that accurately reflected the manner in which work in the professional field would be produced and carried out. This has provided a unique professional development experience that will benefit the students as they progress toward advanced levels of study and, ultimately, as they join a variety of professional fields.

As the new final project of the semester, the three faculty teaching sections of the course integrated the project with their course goals and outcomes. Content for the coloring book, including possible locations and imagery, were presented to the three instructors. They then offered feedback on aesthetics and conceptual approaches to their students, while also challenging them to use their own styles or voices as shown throughout the semester, and their own visions for the application of imagery as a coloring book solution that would engage the widest range of audiences.

As Lowell Isaac, one of the instructors, said: "This project was a good way to talk to my students about the need for an illustrator to maintain their individuality and creativity, within the strict parameters of a given professional illustration job.... An illustrator must be able to expand on the context they are given, and not let themselves be confined by it. As you can see, many of them did exactly that."

We are very proud of the completed coloring book, and we hope that many people can find as much joy in coloring these iconic images of the IUPUI campus and community as our students have found in drawing them.

GREG HULL, INTERIM DEAN
HERRON SCHOOL OF ART AND DESIGN

PARTICIPATING ARTISTS

JULIA ALLEN

ACACIA ANDERSON

SARAH BAILEY

SYDNEY BAILEY

CORA BARNETT

KATIE BECKER

BRITTANY BENTLEY

ALYSSA BOILANGER-DEAN

CHARLIE BOURQUEIN

AILEEN CARRETO

JORDYN CONNELL

DAVID CONNER

TERESA COPENHAVER

ELIAS EVANS

ELLIOT EVANS

MEGAN FISHER

DEZIREE FLORENCE

WYATT FRENCH

BENJI FRICKE

BLISS HARDIN

CAMRYN HATTIEX

RANEEM HIJAZI

JORDAN HILLMAN

LYNDA HOWELL

CAROLINE KRIDLE

EMILY LEMKE

ANDREW MARLATT

GABRIELLE MCNEILL

TAVIA MINTON

KJ MILBURN

SAMANTHA PACIS

EMILY PARKER

MITCHELL POLASKI

CALDER ROBINSON

ANNA SULLIVAN

SOPHIA SAMPLE

RIO SANTOS

KATHRYN SCHOMER

EMMA SCHWARTZ

BRI SQUADRONI

CONNOR STUMP

JOHN VAZQUEZ

GILLIAN WEBB

MATTHEW YANEZ

SCHOOL PRIDE (DETAIL), EMILY PARKER, 2020

PRESS

CANCER RESEARCH INSTITUTE
SOPHIE SAMPLE, 2020

INDIANAPOLIS CULTURAL TRAIL VIEWS
KATIE BECKER, 2020

JOSEPH T. TAYLOR HALL
SAMANTHA PACIS, 2020

PRESS

UNIVERSITY HALL
KJ MILBURN, 2020

ROBERT W. LONG HALL
LYNDA HOWELL, 2020

PRESS

MICHIGAN STREET BRIDGE
BRITTANY BENTLEY, 2020

INTERNATIONAL FESTIVAL AT CAMPUS CENTER
ELIAS EVANS, 2020

PRESS

UNIVERSITY TOWER
CHARLIE BOURQUEIN, 2020

BALL GARDENS AT BALL RESIDENCE HALL
JORDAN HILLMAN, 2020

BALL RESIDENCE HALL
CORA BARNETT, 2020

ROTARY BUILDING
ELLIOT EVANS, 2020

IUPUI REGATTA WHITE RIVER VIEWS
GABRIELLE MCNEILL, 2020

PRESS

SCIENCE AND ENGINEERING LABORATORY BUILDING
SARAH BAILEY, 2020

IU NATATORIUM DAVID
CONNER, 2020

PRESS

BALL RESIDENCE HALL INTERIOR
WYATT FRENCH, 2020

JAWZ
TERESA COPENHAVER, 2020

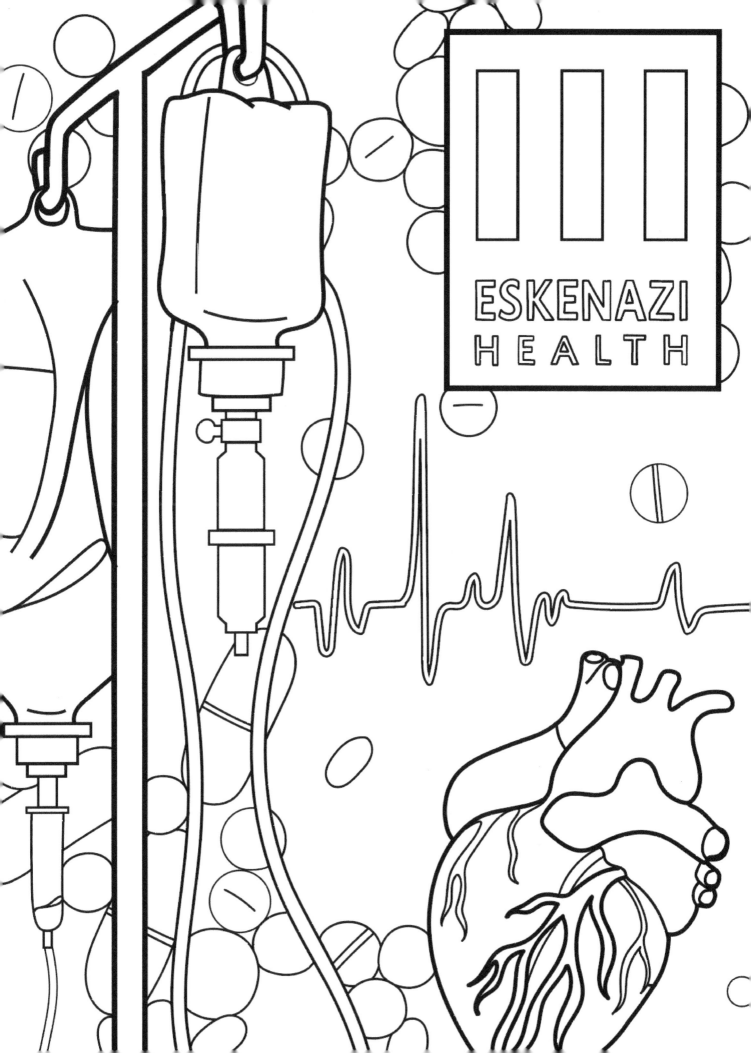

CAVANAUGH HALL COMMUTER TUBE
CALDER ROBINSON, 2020

PRESS

IUPUI REGATTA BENJI
FRICKE, 2020

PRESS

WHITE RIVER PEDESTRIAN BRIDGE
ACACIA ANDERSON, 2020

PRESS

THE SHREVE GATEWAY AT MICHIGAN AND WEST STREETS
RANEEM HIJAZI, 2020

MICHAEL A. CARROLL TRACK AND SOCCER STADIUM
MITCHELL POLASKI, 2020

DIGITAL FABRICATION LAB AT SIDNEY AND LOIS ESKENAZI HALL, HERRON SCHOOL OF ART AND DESIGN
RIO SANTOS, 2020

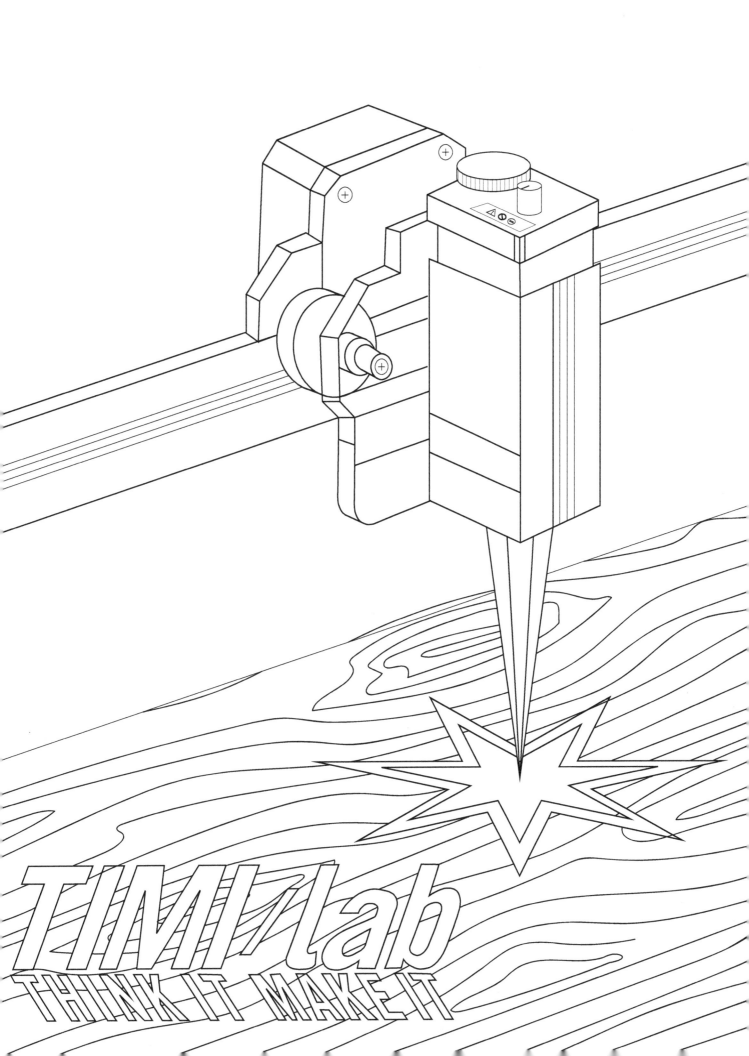

SIDNEY AND LOIS ESKENAZI HALL, HERRON SCHOOL OF ART AND DESIGN
ELIAS EVANS, 2020

PRESS

SIDNEY & LOIS ESKENAZI
FINE ARTS CENTER

LAWRENCE INLOW HALL - IU MCKINNEY SCHOOL OF LAW
SYDNEY BAILEY, 2020

PRESS

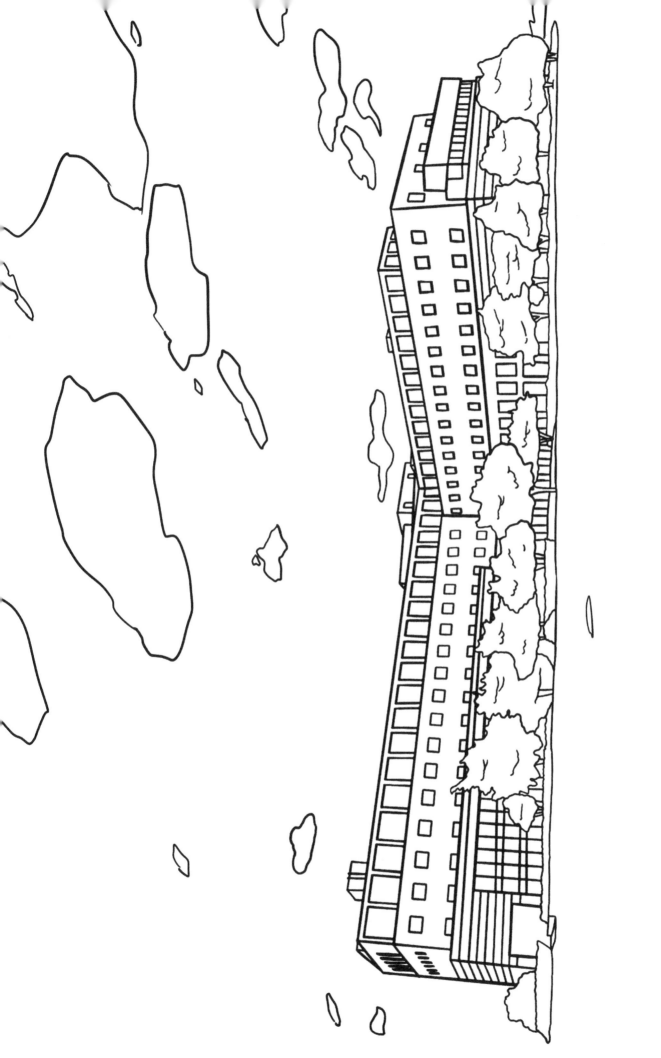

PRESS

CAMPUS MAP
AILEEN CARRETO, 2020

CPSIA information can be obtained
at www.ICGtesting.com
Printed in the USA
LVHW071515130321
681460LV00015B/675